JPIC MacMan
McManis, Margaret Olivia
The wild Texas stampede!

$15.95
ocn212847914
04/20/2009

The Wild
TEXAS
STAMPEDE!

By Margaret McManis
Illustrated by Bruce Dupree

PELICAN PUBLISHING COMPANY
GRETNA 2008

To my new granddaughter, Olivia, and to my mother, Jimmie Olive Marsh, 1923-2008, her creative spirit made me what I am.
—MM

To Claire and Carl
—BD

The word "Pelican" and the depiction of a pelican are trademarks of Pelican Publishing Company, Inc., and are registered in the U.S. Patent and Trademark Office.

Library of Congress Cataloging-in-Publication Data

McManis, Margaret Olivia.
  The wild Texas stampede! / by Margaret McManis ; illustrated by Bruce Dupree.
     p. cm.
  Summary: James Stephen Hogg, the nineteenth-century Texas governor and exotic animal collector, puts his daughter, Ima, in charge of her troublesome younger brother who likes to "bother the buffaloes, outrage the ostriches, and panic the pachyderms."
  ISBN 978-1-58980-568-2 (hardcover : alk. paper) 1. Hogg, Ima—Juvenile fiction. [1. Hogg, Ima—Fiction. 2. Brothers and sisters—Fiction. 3. Behavior—Fiction. 4. Animals—Fiction. 5. Texas—History—1846-1950—Fiction.] I. Dupree, Bruce, ill. II. Title.
  PZ7.M47856Wi 2008
  [E]—dc22

              2008004125

Printed in Korea

Published by Pelican Publishing Company, Inc.
1000 Burmaster Street, Gretna, Louisiana 70053

The Wild Texas Stampede!

Papa told me to mind my little brother.

"But Papa, Tom's more trouble than a lap full of hungry puppies!"

"Now Ima girl, I'm counting on you!" called Papa as he waved goodbye from the seat of the buggy, our new buggy that was to take him to Austin for another election.

Mind my brother! Why, I couldn't even find him most days.

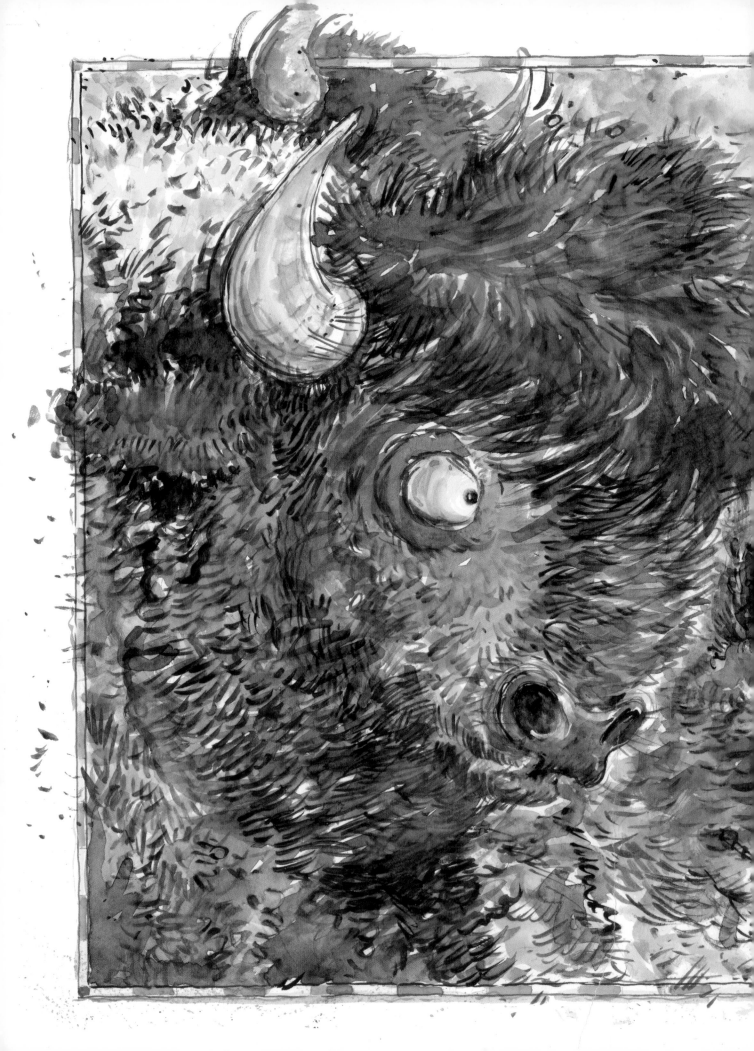

"The buffaloes are a-a-a-fter me!" came a familiar cry from our back pasture. "It's a *stampede!*"

I raced out of the barn just in time to see Tom scramble under the fence. Puffs of sand whipped in dark circles around the hooves of two very angry buffalo bulls.

"Tom, what did you do to them this time? Remember what Papa told you? Don't bother the buffaloes!" How I wished my brothers Will and Mike were here, instead of on a cattle drive. They could always make Tom behave.

"Ima, but there ain't nothin' to do 'round here. It's always, 'Don't bother the buffaloes, don't bother the buffaloes.' Can't a guy have a little fun?"

Papa's buffaloes arrived one dry summer on the train from Jackson Hole, Wyoming. Everyone in Texas knew about Governor Hogg's wonderful menagerie—elephants from India, ostriches from Africa, and now buffalo from Wyoming.

"Hey, I ain't gonna hurt Papa's big hairy cows," Tom said the next morning after breakfast. "I just wanted to see if I could git me up a good bullfight. They don't like red, ya know, so I'm gonna buy a big red bandana just for fun."

"Red bandana or blue bonnet. Guess it can't be any worse than the time you tied my bonnet to our old sow."

"Or the time I cut the fingers off your best gloves and you couldn't ride your horse for a week."

I had forgotten about that little joke. Now I was madder than a bee-stung heifer. It was gosh-awful hard to mind my brother, but Papa would be depending on me.

"Brother, boy," I yelled as he sprinted out the front door. "Someday you're gonna bite off more than you can chew. Then watch out, *you'll* be buffalo stew!"

Minutes later I heard a furious barking coming from the direction of the corral, and there was my terrier, Tippy, jumping up and down beside a big sorghum barrel.

Balanced atop the barrel stood Tom. In his hand was Papa's pocket watch. In the corral were Jack and Jill, our ostriches. As he swung the watch slowly back and forth, the dizzy birds swayed like Maypoles in the morning breeze.

"For Pete's sake," I shouted. "Don't outrage the ostriches!"

"Aw, I ain't gonna hurt those goofy drumstick birds. I'm just sportin' with 'em."

Later that night, Tom wolfed down a glass of fresh buttermilk and cornbread for dinner. "Hey, Ima," he began, "tomorrow I'm gonna teach Tippy some circus tricks, with the pachyderms. Man, I love those elepha—!"

"Grrrr, yip, yip, yip!" Suddenly Tippy scrambled after a big mouse behind our kitchen table. Quicker than a Texas rattler, I grabbed the mouse and swung it in front of Tom's face.

"Don't you even think about it, Brother! This mouse and those elephants will never ever meet each other."

"Yeah, Ima, I know, I know, 'Don't panic the pachyderms!'"

The next day, I heard news of the election in Austin and knew Papa would be home soon, but not soon enough for me. At breakfast, my brother grabbed a warm biscuit dripping with sorghum syrup and made a beeline for the pasture.

"Don't bother the . . . " I called.

"Yeah, yeah, I know," he shouted back. "Don't bother the buffaloes, don't outrage the ostriches, *and don't panic the pachyderms.*"

Lunchtime brought unhappy bellowing from the back pasture.

"Oh, bother, not again," I shouted as the screen door slammed behind me. I worried as black and white feathers swirled in nervous circles around my head. Was it time to panic? Angry buffalo dust appeared on the horizon. It was time to panic!

"It's a *stampede!*"

Out in front of the maddened herd raced my brother, a bright red bandana sticking out of his back pocket and a wide grin on his dirt-covered face.

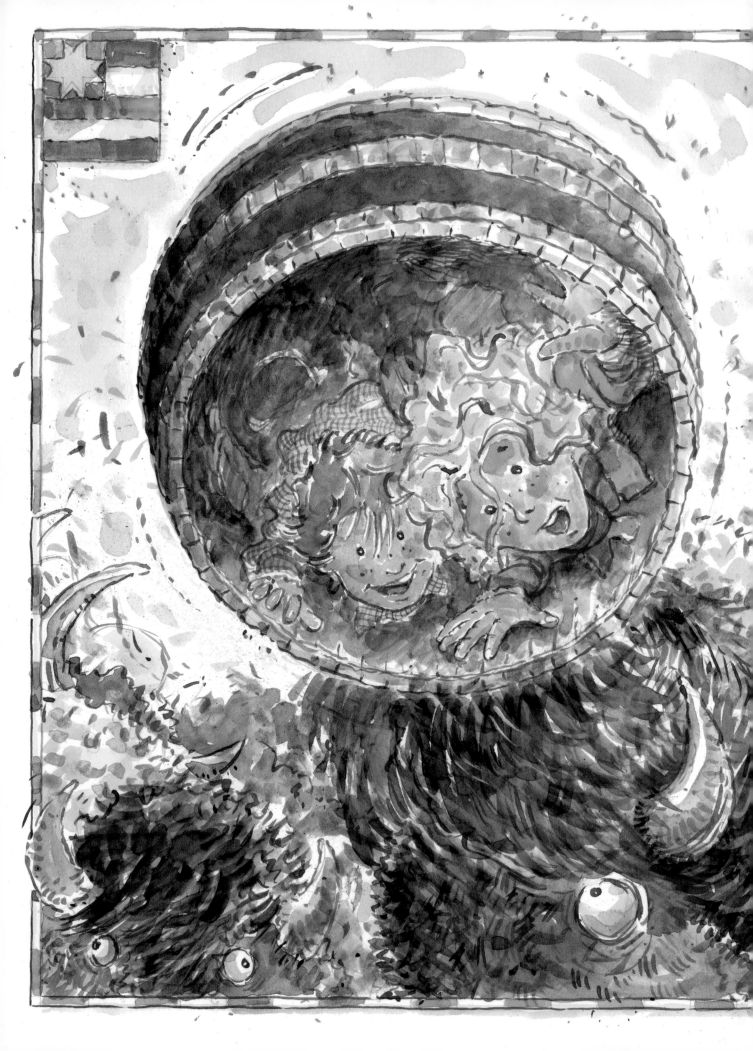

I grabbed our old sorghum barrel from the corral and rolled it with all my might into the center of the pasture. Then I jumped inside. As Tom sprinted toward the fence, I grabbed his coveralls and pulled him in with me.

Kaboom! It felt as if a locomotive hit the side of the barrel. We rolled over and over. Then my brother and I peered out at an incredible sight. My tiny terrier had the biggest bull by the nose, refusing to let go and growling like a timber wolf. Finally all the stampeding animals came to the edge of the fence and settled down. Tippy released the nose of the bull and dashed under the fence.

"Man, that was great, Ima! What *fun!* Let's do that again."

My face turned the color of Tom's bandana this time. "Are you crazy? We almost got stampeded to death!"

"Hey, Ima," he replied with a grin. "Don't you know? *Almost* don't count!"

But Papa was depending on me to take care of my brother, so later that night, under the glow of a full moon, I hitched our old mule to the wagon and led him out to the center of the pasture to the old sorghum barrel.

In the back of the wagon stood a barrel. Inside the barrel was a sticky surprise. As I poured the tarlike syrup from one barrel to the other, a wide grin spread across my face.

The next day Tippy and I sat as quiet as cupboard mice, watching Tom's stampede. My brother sprinted toward the barrel with a smile on his face and glee in his voice, but it changed to a panicked, outraged bellow as he sank into the thick black syrup.

"Hey, Tom," I called from the fence post. *"And don't forget! Never swim in the sorghum syrup!"*

HISTORICAL NOTE

The Hogg family of Texas did indeed have a wonderful menagerie. Governor Hogg loved taking his children to the Mollie Bailey Circus when it was in town and even collected exotic animals, including two ostriches. Ima Hogg never had a sister named Ura Hogg, but she did have three troublesome brothers. Will was seven years older than Ima and grew up to become a lawyer and philanthropist in Houston, Texas, while Mike, who was three years younger than Ima, helped his sister build the family mansion called Bayou Bend.

Tom, who was five years younger than Ima and the youngest, proved to be the most troublesome in real life. While the family lived in the governor's mansion in Austin, he created havoc for Papa and Ima. Since their mother had died when Ima was thirteen, she was often left in charge of her younger siblings. Once while sliding down the banister of the spiral staircase in the mansion, something strictly forbidden by Papa, Tom fell off and broke his arm. To this day when you visit the governor's mansion, you can still observe the holes that were left in the lovely cherry staircase banister after Governor Hogg hammered nails into it over one hundred and fifty years ago to keep his youngest son from ever performing the feat again. This fact gave me the idea for the story of Ima and her troublesome little brother who loved to "bother the buffaloes, outrage the ostriches, and panic the pachyderms."